■■SCHOLASTIC

Teaching Reading With
Bill Martin Books

BY CONSTANCE J. LEUENBERGER

NEW YORK • TORONTO • LONDON • AUCKLAND • SYDNEY
MEXICO CITY • NEW DELHI • HONG KONG • BUENOS AIRES

Teaching
Resources

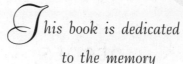

This book is dedicated
to the memory
of Renee Lynn Remer.

❧

"I think I'll miss you most of all."
—DOROTHY TO THE SCARECROW IN *THE WIZARD OF OZ*

ACKNOWLEDGMENTS

*I would like to give special thanks to my editor, Joan Novelli, and to Deborah Schecter
for making this book what it is. Many thanks also to all my friends and family,
who have continually supported me in this writing endeavor!*

Cover from BROWN BEAR, BROWN BEAR, WHAT DO YOU SEE? illustrated by Eric Carle, text by Bill Martin Jr. Cover illustration copyright © 1992 by Eric Carle. Reprinted by permission of Henry Holt and Company, LLC.

Cover from CHICKA, CHICKA BOOM BOOM reprinted with the permission of Simon & Schuster Books for Young Readers, an imprint of Simon & Schuster Children's Publishing Division from CHICKA, CHICKA BOOM BOOM by Bill Martin Jr. and John Archambault, illustrated by Lois Ehlert. Illustrations copyright © 1989 by Lois Ehlert.

Cover from THE HAPPY HIPPOPOTAMI by Bill Martin Jr., illustrated by Betsy Everitt. Illustrations copyright © 1991 by Betsy Everitt. Reprinted by permission of Harcourt Inc.

Photo of Bill Martin, Jr.: courtesy of Henry Holt, Sigrid Estrada

"The Folk Who Live in Backward Town" from THE LLAMA WHO HAD NO PAJAMA: 100 FAVORITE POEMS. Copyright © 1959 and renewed 1987 by Mary Ann Hoberman. Reprinted by permission of Harcourt, Inc.

"Here Comes the Band" by William Cole. Reprinted by permission of the Estate of William Cole.

"Rain Poem" by Elizabeth Coatsworth. Copyright © 1957 by Macmillan Publishing.

"Rhinos Purple, Hippos Green" from BREAKFAST, BOOKS, & DREAMS by Michael Patrick Hearn. Copyright © 1981 by Michael Patrick Hearn. Published by Frederick Warner.

"Something Is There" from BEWARE, TAKE CARE: SPOOKY POEMS OF LILIAN MOORE. Copyright © 2006 by the Estate of Lilian Moore. Reprinted by permission of Henry Holt and Company, LLC.

Every effort has been made to contact copyright holders for permission to reproduce borrowed material. The publisher regrets any oversights that may have occurred and will be pleased to rectify them in subsequent reprints of the work.

Edited by Joan Novelli
Cover and interior design by Kathy Massaro
Interior art by James Graham Hale

ISBN-13: 978-0-439-60963-0
ISBN-10: 0-439-60963-1

2 3 4 5 6 7 8 9 10   40   14 13 12 11 10 09 08 07

Contents

About This Book

Although Bill Martin Jr. says there were no books in his home while he was growing up, and he was not a reader, he was drawn to words on a page: "Even when type on a page didn't make sense to me, I considered myself a reader—because I loved the sound and the cadence of the language, the power of narrative, and the images words concocted in my mind." (www.friend.ly.net/scoop/biographies/martinbill/index.html) His love of language shines through in the dozens of books Bill Martin Jr. has written and coauthored. Young readers delight in the playful, poetic language that abounds in his books. With words like "mishy mushy muddy puddle" (from *Listen to the Rain*, coauthored with John Archambault), "hippoholiday," "hippopotapilots," and "poppasicles" (from *The Happy Hippopotami*), and "Skit skat skoodle doot" (from *Chicka Chicka Boom Boom*, coauthored with John Archambault), Bill Martin Jr.'s books are an irresistible celebration of language.

This book offers an array of lessons that support learning across the curriculum, with a focus on teaching reading. In the pages that follow, you'll find dozens of fresh and creative activities to help children master essential reading skills in the following areas:

◉ "Before Reading" activities invite children to activate background knowledge, make predictions, ask questions, make connections, build vocabulary, and more.

◉ Activities that focus on predictable text and picture clues help children develop important strategies for making sense of text.

◉ To support comprehension, "After Reading" activities explore character development, setting, and plot (including sequencing), and provide practice with retelling. With sample questions to guide their thinking, children are encouraged to make inferences about events and relate what they read to their own experiences.

◉ "Word Play" activities encourage children's natural love of language, taking a close look at word choice (including rhyme, rhythmic language, and use of predictable text), text features, and poetic devices (such as onomatopoeia).

Additional activities for each book enrich learning in writing, math, science, dramatic play, art, musical expression, and much more!

Assessment Suggestions

During a thematic unit it's important to use several different assessments, depending on the children and the activity or project they are involved with. A couple of suggestions follow:

◎ **Rubrics and Checklists of Desired Behaviors:** Rubrics and checklists, including self-assessments, make it easy to document children's project work. Repeating a rubric over the course of a thematic unit or project provides a record of growth.

◎ **Sticky Note Assessment Folders:** Place a sticky note for each child in a folder. Use the sticky notes to jot down anecdotal records related to assessment. This makes it convenient to gather assessment information while observing and working with children. Transfer the notes to children's individual folders for a record of their work during a lesson, activity, or project.

Name _____ Date _____

Assessment Checklist

Skills	Skill Mastered	Skill at Emergent Level	Skill Not Yet Demonstrated
Asks questions while reading.			
Uses pictures in the book as sequencing clues.			
Uses vocabulary for time order.			
Provides details that support main idea.			

Support for the Language Arts Standards

The activities in this book are designed to support the following standards outlined by the Mid-continent Research for Education and Learning (McREL), an organization that collects and synthesizes national and state K–12 curriculum standards.

Uses the general skills and strategies of the reading process:

◆ Understands how print is organized and read

◆ Creates mental images from pictures and print

◆ Uses meaning clues to aid comprehension and make predictions about content

Uses reading skills and strategies to understand and interpret a variety of literary texts:

◆ Uses reading skills and strategies to understand a variety of familiar literary passages and texts, including fiction

◆ Knows main ideas or theme, setting, main characters, main events, sequence, and problems in stories

◆ Makes simple inferences regarding the order of events and possible outcomes

◆ Relates stories to personal experiences

Uses the general skills and strategies of the writing process:

◆ Uses writing and other methods to describe familiar persons, places, objects, or experiences

◆ Writes in a variety of forms or genres, including responses to literature

Kendall, J. S., & Marzano, R. J. (2004). *Content knowledge: A compendium of standards and benchmarks for K–12 education.* Aurora, CO: Mid-continent Research for Education and Learning. Online database: http://www.mcrel.org/standards-benchmarks/

Meet Bill Martin Jr.

When Bill Martin Jr.'s brother was injured at the end of World War II, he asked Bill to write a story that he could illustrate as he recovered. Bill Martin Jr. wrote *The Little Squeegy Bug* in 1943, and his brother illustrated it. Published in 1945, *The Little Squeegy Bug* launched Bill Martin Jr.'s career.

When the celebrated author speaks of his career, he says, "A blessed thing happened to me as a child. I had a teacher who read to me. Of course, she was reading to all the other children in the classroom, but I believed she was reading *just to me* because I was a nonreader." (www.friend.ly.net/scoop/biographies/martinbill/index.html) Bill Martin Jr. goes on to explain that he was 20 years old before he actually read. He was admitted to college and masked his reading disability, while teachers thought he was lazy or unprepared. Today Bill Martin Jr. says he doesn't write books but talks them. He wants to hear the sound of the language before he writes the words on paper. The teacher who first read to him tuned his ears to the voice of texts, as he explains, "not to the voice of Robert Louis Stevenson, but to the voice of *Treasure Island*." (www.friend.ly.net/scoop/biographies/martinbill/index.html)

According to Bill Martin Jr., he wrote *Brown Bear, Brown Bear, What Do You See?* on the Long Island Rail Road between stops. It took him just 33 minutes. He muttered lines out loud and tried out the language and rhythm of the story as the train rolled along, much to the surprise of fellow travelers. He says, "I saw what children were able to do with that story, and I became more courageous in creating rhythmic, highly patterned stories." (www.billmartinjr.com) Those stories have become the ones that children know and love and return to again and again.

Activities for Any Time

Use the following literature-based lessons to enhance, extend, and illuminate students' learning with any of the Bill Martin Jr. titles featured in this book.

Planning an Author Study

Many of Martin's books lend themselves to enhancing a topic of study—for example, *Brown Bear, Brown Bear, What Do You See?* reinforces color recognition and vocabulary during a color unit. *Chicka Chicka Boom Boom* is a welcome addition to any alphabet study. However, you and your students may want to delve deeper into the works of Bill Martin Jr. and create an author study as part of your classroom activities. Gather all the Bill Martin Jr. titles you can and share the books with children over the course of three or four weeks. Decorate a bulletin board and use it to feature covers, characters' names, and favorite quotes from Bill Martin Jr.'s books, as well as children's projects based on the various lessons in this book. Invite students to try their hands at writing snappy pieces of language that roll off their tongue. Encourage ongoing discussion of the books with the following questions:

◎ How are the books of Bill Martin Jr. alike? How are they different?

◎ If you were going to give an award to one Bill Martin Jr. book, which would you choose? Why?

◎ Which of Bill Martin's books do you think are serious? Which do you think are silly?

◎ What type of books do you think Bill Martin Jr. likes to write best?

◎ What's fun for you about the language in Bill Martin Jr.'s books?

Playing With Poetry

Bill Martin Jr. says he doesn't write books; he "talks" them. He always begins his writing by talking through a story many times. His work proves this true, as his books have such rhythmic, almost poetic, language. As children read *Listen to the Rain* or *The Happy Hippopotami* again and again, they reap the rewards of poetry while developing their understanding of print. Keeping this in mind, take as many opportunities as possible to play with poetry in your classroom. Try some of these ideas:

Poetry Center: Stock the center with anthologies and collections of poetry, books that have poetic language, charts of poems, and poetry on tape. Invite children to experience poetry and then write some of their own. Be sure to include paper, markers, crayons, and other materials for writing and illustrating poetry.

(continued)

Morning Poem: Start off each day with a poem! Write a poem on chart paper and add it to the easel in the morning circle. Each morning, read the poem together as a class. Children can revisit the poem on their own, building word recognition skills as well as their sense of rhythm, rhyme, and other poetic devices.

Poetry Notebooks: Give each child a notebook for storing poetry. Encourage children to copy poems they enjoy in their notebooks. Children can also try their own hand at poetry, and include some of their own poems.

Poetry Readings: Plan a formal poetry reading with your class. Allow children to show their artistic interpretations of poems by sharing a dramatic reading. Invite parents and other classes to share this special event.

Readers Theater

Many of Bill Martin Jr.'s books just beg to be read aloud. Readers Theater is the perfect place for this, allowing children to develop an appreciation for literature and drama. Create simple scripts based on passages of the books, and let children act them out in small groups. If children are uncomfortable with the scripted format, invite them to read aloud from a book with great expression.

Take-Home Books in a Bag

Bring the wonderful literature of Bill Martin Jr. into students' homes! Fill a large, resealable plastic bag (or a small tote or backpack) with a Bill Martin Jr. book and six or seven activities based on the book that children and their families can complete together. Send home bags on a rotating basis (in place of homework).

Authors and Illustrators Studio

Create an area in the classroom where children can write and illustrate books. Stock the center with plenty of books by Bill Martin Jr. for inspiration and modeling (both for writing and illustrating), as well as assorted writing materials. Suggested materials include: books by Bill Martin Jr., different types and sizes of paper, markers and crayons, glue and tape, hole punch and stapler, sight word lists, alphabet chart, and picture dictionaries.

Brown Bear, Brown Bear, What Do You See?

(HENRY HOLT, 1983)

"**B**rown Bear, Brown Bear, what do you see? I see a red bird looking at me." This celebrated classic is a favorite for all ages. Readers first meet Brown Bear, followed by Red Bird, Yellow Duck, Blue Horse, Green Frog, Purple Cat, White Dog, Black Sheep, Goldfish, Teacher, and Children. Rhyming and predictable text combined with tissue paper collage illustration makes this a delight for young readers.

Before Reading

Brown Bear Patterns

Introduce the story by taking a quick class poll. Ask: "Who knows this book?" It's likely that many children not only will be familiar with it but will rank it among their favorites. While browsing the book with children, invite them to share what they see. Do they notice a pattern in the book? Is it easy for them to read? What clues can they use to decode the words in the book? Encourage children to join in as you read.

After Reading

Ask the following questions to encourage children to use their predicting skills:

◎ Did you know which animal was coming next in the text? What were some clues that helped you know?

◎ Do you think Bill Martin Jr. should have included a picture clue on each page to help the reader identify the next animal? How would the book be different then?

Poetry Pause

Give each child a copy of the poem "Rhinos Purple, Hippos Green" (page 12). Read the poem together. Encourage a discussion about depicting animals in silly colors, as Eric Carle does in *Brown Bear, Brown Bear, What Do You See?* and as Michael Patrick Hearn does in the poem. Why do authors depict animals in nontraditional colors? When is it a good idea to do this, and when is it a better idea to use the natural colors of animals? Have children complete the activities on the reproducible page to learn more.

Tip

For children just learning to read, the predictable text of *Brown Bear, Brown Bear, What Do You See?* makes them feel as if they are instant readers. For children revisiting reading after a long summer, skills are easily remembered.

Word Play

Brown Bear, Brown Bear, What Do You See? is a great book to read on the first day of school—but it also lends itself well to playing with language any time of year! After reading the book through once or twice, try these activities:

- Invite students to chime in while you read the predictable text. They will have fun predicting and naming each animal that comes next. As children follow along, invite them to use voices that sound like the different animals on each page. For example, Brown Bear might have a very loud, growly voice, and Purple Cat may "meow" as she says, "I see a white dog looking at me."

- Divide the class into color groups to match each animal in the book. For example, anyone wearing red represents Red Bird; anyone wearing yellow would represent Yellow Duck. (If there are colors missing, children can hold colored construction paper.) Retell the story focusing on the color words. When children hear the color they represent, invite them to stand and join in.

Brown Bear, Brown Bear, All Mixed Up! (Language Arts)

Brown Bear's all mixed up! Strengthen children's sequencing skills and vocabulary for time order by putting events from *Brown Bear, Brown Bear, What Do You See?* in order.

- Write each sentence from the book on a sentence strip. Place in random order in a pocket chart.

- Tell children that the story *Brown Bear, Brown Bear, What Do You See?* is all mixed up and needs to be put back together in the correct order.

- Have children place the sentence strips in order to retell the story. Look for opportunities to teach retelling strategies—for example, using the pictures in the book as sequencing clues. For additional sequencing support, color-code each sentence strip (by using the corresponding color marker or gluing a square of construction paper on the sentence strip) to match the characters' colors.

- Invite children to draw pictures of each character to match the sentence strips.

- Display the sentence strips and pictures as a learning center for children to use independently or with partners.

A Brown Bear Necklace (Language Arts, Art)

Children love to make necklaces. Here's one they can make to help retell this favorite story.

- Cut tagboard into 3- by 3-inch squares. Each child will need 11 squares.

- On each square, have children draw an event/animal from the book. (They can write a number on the back of each square to correspond to the sequence of story events.)

- Punch a hole at the top of each square and have children string their pictures on yarn in the order they appear in the book. (A bead in between each square helps to make the necklace more attractive and easier to read and use.)

- Tie the yarn to secure.

- Children can use these necklaces to help retell the story, reinforcing sequencing and oral language skills!

Brown Bear Character Graph

(Math, Language Arts)

Use *Brown Bear, Brown Bear, What Do You See?* to explore characters and reinforce graphing skills.

◎ Invite children to name the characters in *Brown Bear, Brown Bear, What Do You See?* Use the names to set up a bar graph.

◎ Cut construction paper into squares. Choose colors that match those in the book (brown, red, yellow, blue, green, purple, white, black, and gold).

◎ Invite students to choose a construction paper square in the color that represents their favorite character. Have them write their name on the paper and place it on the graph in the appropriate section.

◎ When the graph is complete, stretch students' mathematical thinking by asking questions, such as "How many more people liked Red Bird than Purple Cat? Which character did our class like the most?"

Where Do You Live? What Do You See?

(Language Arts, Social Studies)

Use *Brown Bear, Brown Bear, What Do You See?* to begin a study about your community.

◎ Make or obtain a large map of the state (or city/town/county) where your students live. Take field trips and invite guest speakers into the classroom to learn more about your community and its focal points.

◎ Read aloud informational books and articles to help children learn more about their community. Discuss what makes your community special.

◎ After gathering information, fill in the map of the area, marking points of interest.

◎ Using interactive writing, create a class book about your community. Use *Brown Bear, Brown Bear, What Do You See?* as a model. (See example, above.)

◎ Incorporate Brown Bear into your curriculum all year long. Start the year by making a book that features your new class—for example, "Kindergartners, Kindergartners, What Do You See?" Place a photo of a student on each page with a caption that follows the Brown Bear text pattern. ("Cole, Cole what do you see?" and on the next page "I see Emily looking at me.") Continue this theme to support a study of the seasons ("Pumpkin, Pumpkin, What Do You See?") and topics of special interest ("Penguin, Penguin, What Do You See?").

Rhinos Purple, Hippos Green

My sister says

I shouldn't color

Rhinos purple,

Hippos green.

She says

I shouldn't be so stupid;

Those are things

She's never seen.

But I don't care

What my sister says,

I don't care

What my sister's seen.

I will color

What I want to—

Rhinos purple,

Hippos green.

— by Michael Patrick Hearn

What color would you choose for rhinos and hippos? Fill in the words to retell the end of the poem. Color the pictures.

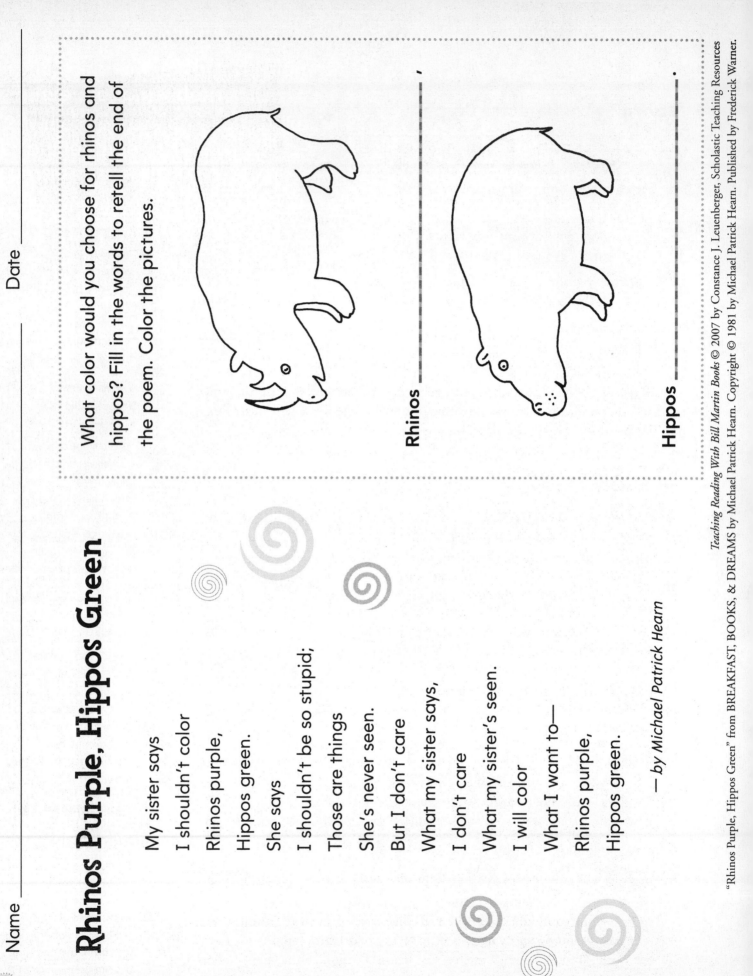

Rhinos _____

Hippos _____

Teaching Reading With Bill Martin Books © 2007 by Constance J. Leuenberger, Scholastic Teaching Resources

Barn Dance!

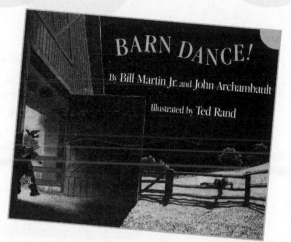

(HENRY HOLT, 1986)

Come along to the barn where the animals are do-si-do-ing and having a foot stompin', barnyard rompin' good time. The story begins in the quiet of the night as a young boy sneaks out to the barn, and with the cadence of a square dance caller, the story of a rollicking barn dance unfolds. The story quietly ends the way it started, with the boy sneaking back into the house in the wee hours of the morning.

Before Reading

Making Predictions

Show students the cover of the book. Invite them to share what they think is happening in the illustration. Explain that this story is about a boy who sneaks into his barn in the middle of the night and finds something funny going on with the animals. Invite students to share what they think animals do when humans aren't watching. Ask questions, such as "Do animals act like people? How do animals have fun?"

After Reading

Looking at the illustrations in the book can help children feel as though they are really outside in the middle of the night. Use the following questions to help children make connections to the book:

◎ Have you ever been outside late at night with the moonlight shining bright?

◎ When you look at the illustrations in the text, does the night look scary or inviting?

◎ Would you like to be invited to a barnyard dance such as the one in the book? Would you be excited to go, or a little scared?

Sample Square Dancing Steps

Circle Family: Dancers form a circle and join hands. They face slightly left or right and move around the circle in a clockwise or counterclockwise motion.

Do-si-do: Dancers advance and pass right shoulders. Without turning, each dancer moves to the right passing in back of the other dancer. Then, moving backward, each passes left shoulders, returning to starting position.

Arm Turns: To complete a "left-arm turn," dancers join left forearms and walk forward around each other the distance specified—for example, half (180°), three quarters (270°), and full (360°). A "right-arm turn" is completed in a similar manner, except dancers turn with the right forearm.

Mr. Scarecrow (Language Arts)

The scarecrow in *Barn Dance!* is a fiddle player. Ask students what they would think of a scarecrow that could walk, dance, sing, and talk. Invite them to think of other stories they have seen or heard where the scarecrow can do things like this. Then encourage children to read this fun poem as you play a name recognition game.

> Mr. Scarecrow,
> Oh, Mr. Scarecrow,
> You're as scary as can be!
> You scared Evan ,
> And you also scared me!

◎ Write the following chant on chart paper, leaving a blank space as shown to fill in each student's name.

> Mr. Scarecrow,
> Oh, Mr. Scarecrow, you're as scary as can be!
> You scared _____ ,
> And you also scared me!

◎ Write each child's name on a sentence strip. Trim to size.

◎ Place a piece of Velcro on the chart where the name will appear and on the back of each sentence strip.

◎ Invite children to take turns reciting the poem, inserting a classmate's name in the blank.

◎ When a name is called, that child gets to take a turn choosing another name for the blank on the chart.

Square Dancing

(Language Arts, Social Studies, Music, Movement)

Square dancing is a part of our American heritage, and it's a lot of fun too. Bring some square dancing into the classroom to help students gain a deeper appreciation for the book's topic.

◎ Invite a local square dancing club to visit your classroom and share information about square dancing, including its history and some of the simpler calls (such as "circle left/right," "forward/back," and "do-si-do").

◎ Let students join in and practice a few steps in the classroom. (See Sample Square Dancing Steps, left.) Play some square dancing music to complete the experience. The following are just a few of the songs used in square dancing: "The City of New Orleans," "Hey Good Lookin'," "Bare Necessities," "Mickey Mouse Club March," and "Zip-a-Dee-Doo-Dah."

Barnyard Math (Math)

Children practice math (operations and problem-solving) and listening skills while creating a barn dance of their own.

◎ Give children a copy of the barn (page 16) and animals (page 17). Let children color the barn and animals. Have them cut out the animals. (If you have enough toy barnyard animals, you can use them instead.)

◎ Make up and share number stories about the animals in the barn. Have children add and subtract animals from their barn to show the answers. For example, you might say:

"The barn had three cows in it, but one went out to eat some grass. How many cows are in the barn now?"

◎ Invite students to pair up and trade their own number stories to solve.

Word Play

Reread passages from *Barn Dance!* that incorporate dialect. For example:

**The scarecrow tucked the fiddle underneath his chin
An' fiddled out a welcome to all his country kin.
He fiddled through the woods 'n' fields 'n' all aroun' the farm,
Biddin' ever'body come to a hoedown in the barn.**

Explain to students that a dialect is a regional variety of language that differs from standard speech.

● On chart paper (or a whiteboard), write some of the dialect phrases. Account for the use of apostrophes in the words, explaining that apostrophes are used to show missing letters in a word. Guide students in figuring out which letters are missing. Write the standard spellings next to those from the book.

Book Links

Going to Sleep on the Farm
by Wendy Cheyette Lewison
(Dial, 1992)

Before going to bed, a young boy spends the last few moments of play with his toy farm animals. As the boy's father explains to him that all the farm animals are going to sleep, the boy becomes more and more drowsy.

In the Moonlight, Waiting
by Carol Carrick
(Clarion, 1990)

In the spring of the year, a young girl wakes to find her mother in the barn assisting with the birth of a new lamb.

Owl Moon
by Jane Yolen
(Philomel, 1987)

In this Caldecott Medal winner, peaceful illustrations of a snow-covered landscape capture the wonder of childhood adventures in a dark forest.

Parents in the Pigpen, Pig in the Tub
by Amy Ehrlich
(Dial, 1993)

When the barnyard animals move into the main house and begin to demand all the comforts of household living, the humans eventually flee to the barnyard abode.

Name _____

Date _____

Barnyard Math

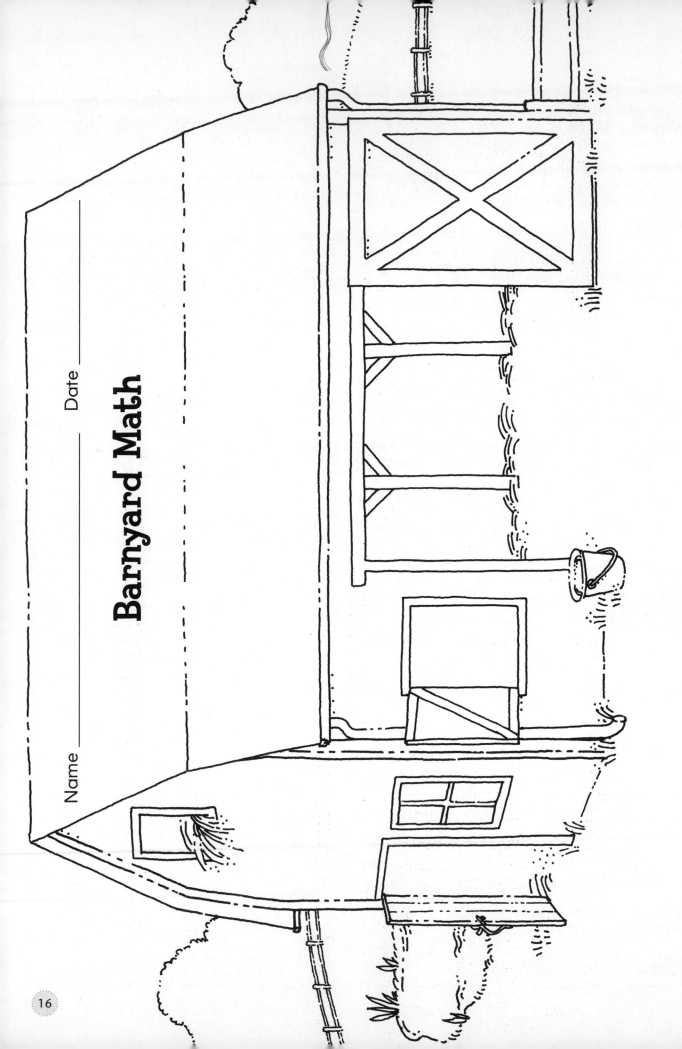

Teaching Reading With Bill Martin Books © 2007 by Constance J. Leuenberger, Scholastic Teaching Resources

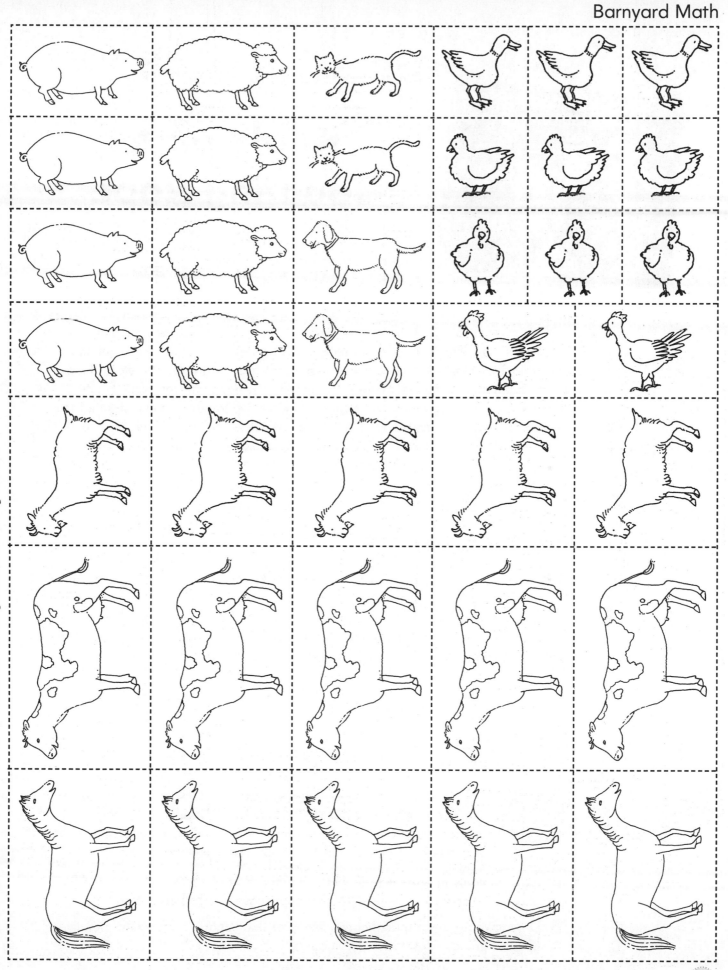

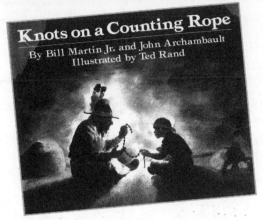

Knots on a Counting Rope

(HENRY HOLT, 1987)

This poignant story, set in the American Southwest, tells about the bond between a Native American boy and his grandfather, who uses a counting rope to tell the story about the night his grandson was born. As the grandfather tells the story of the stormy night and the birth of the sickly, frail baby, the boy continues to ask questions about his life. The staccato dialogue continues while the grandfather explains that the boy has "raced darkness and won," letting readers know the boy is blind. The hope, love, and courage in this story cross all boundaries and are felt universally.

Before Reading

Storytelling Traditions

Talk about stories people tell that aren't written down. Children might like to share snippets of such stories their families or others have shared with them. These might be stories grandparents tell about "the old days," legends about the weather or other everyday subjects, even stories about when children were babies. Explain that stories that are not written down and are handed down from generation to generation are called oral traditions. Point out that *Knots on a Counting Rope* is a story in which a grandfather hands down oral traditions, or stories, to his grandson.

After Reading

The grandfather in this story was very wise. He was a marvelous storyteller who used this ability to help his grandson cope with blindness. Use the following questions to guide children in exploring the relationship between these important characters:

◎ How do you think the grandfather and grandson feel about each other? What are some clues in the words? What are some clues in the pictures?

◎ Do you think the grandfather was trying to share another important message with his grandson? What is that message?

Telling My Story (Language Arts)

Everyone has a story to tell! Invite children to share an event that has happened to them and how that event changed their life in some way. Encourage children to use pictures and words to tell their story. Younger children can dictate their stories. Share these prompts to encourage children in their writing:

- Let children revisit the book to find out when the boy was given the name "Boy-Strength-of-Blue-Horses."

- Why was this name chosen for the boy?

- Is there a reason your name was given to you?

- Boy-Strength-of-Blue-Horses learned to adapt to his blindness with the help of his horse and his grandfather. Are there ways in which you have learned how to do something differently? Why? How did it work out?

Make a Counting Rope (Math, Social Studies, Language Arts)

Draw children's attention to the counting rope in the illustrations throughout the book. Share that each knot on the rope represents a different part of the grandfather's story. Introduce the word *quipu* (KEE-pōo), the term used by the Inca for the system of knotted cords they used to record information. Like the counting rope in the story, the placement of knots in a quipu represented different items or events. Invite children to create their own quipus or counting ropes.

- Give each child a length of ribbon (to serve as their counting rope). Have children tie a knot in their ribbon to represent each year of their life.

- Then ask children to think about something significant for each year. (Or have them tie a knot for each significant event they remember, regardless of the year it happened—for example, a knot for moving to a new town, having a new brother, starting kindergarten, and loosing a first tooth.)

- Encourage children to share their counting ropes in small groups, taking turns touching each knot and telling something about that year (or time) in their life.

Book Links

Now One Foot, Now the Other
by Tomie dePaola
(Putnam, 1981)

When Bobby's grandfather suffers a stroke, Bobby teaches him to walk, just as his grandfather taught him as a child. This heartwarming book captures the beauty of human relationships.

The Two of Them
by Aliki
(HarperCollins, 1979)

"The day she was born, her grandfather made her a ring of silver and polished stone, because he loved her already." As the years pass by and fill with happy times at the beach, in the mountains, and working at the grandfather's store, the grandfather is always there to take care of the girl. When he grows sick, she is there to care for him.

When I Was Young in the Mountains
by Cynthia Rylant
(Dutton, 1982)

This Caldecott Honor book brings back the nostalgia of a childhood spent in the West Virginia mountains with grandparents, swimming in the swimming hole, taking baths in the kitchen, and drinking cocoa. The spare, repetitive text is a beautiful ode to simpler times.

Thank You (Social Studies, Language Arts)

The boy and the grandfather in *Knots on a Counting Rope* had a very special relationship. The grandfather always seemed to be looking out for and helping his grandson. Use this activity to help children consider special relationships in their lives.

◎ Begin by discussing in what ways the grandfather is important to the boy. Encourage children to use details from the story to support their ideas. Then invite students to think of someone who is important to them. This might be a family member, a cafeteria worker who helps them open their milk every day at lunchtime, a friend, or a favorite neighbor.

◎ Discuss ways people let others know they appreciate them—for example, people send thank-you notes when someone does something nice for them.

◎ Provide construction paper and other art supplies for children to make cards. Have them write or dictate a message of thanks to someone special in their lives.

◎ When the cards are complete, students can distribute them to the people they would like to thank. (For children who want to thank a faraway special person, check into mailing the card.)

Word Play

Although Bill Martin Jr. never specifically points out who is talking in this book, the reader is always sure which person is speaking. Invite students to study the text with you and notice the indentations that help the reader understand who is speaking. Let students practice reading the lines (chorally or individually) and using the text format on the page to help them read fluently. Compare the text in this book to the text in other picture books. Notice other examples in books where the placement of the words on the page is unusual.

Listen to the Rain

◆◆

(HENRY HOLT, 1988)

Listen to the Rain
By Bill Martin Jr. and John Archambault
Illustrated by James Endicott

"Listen to the rain, the whisper of the rain, the slow soft sprinkle, the drip-drop tinkle, the first wet whisper of the rain." So begins this lyrical tale of a rainstorm. The story unfolds through rhythmic language and powerful illustrations, as the rainstorm quietly begins, storms to a roaring climax, and softly comes to a delicate stop.

Before Reading

Rainy Day Feelings

Rainy days and nights can mean very different things to different people. Invite children to discuss how they feel on a rainy day or night. How do they feel when they hear rain? Scared? Cozy? Sleepy? Why? How do they feel when they have the chance to go puddle jumping on a rainy day?

After Reading

Discussion "Starters"

The rhythmic language of this story is mesmerizing. After sharing the story, revisit some of the language to explore word choice.

◎ As the story progresses, readers do feel as if they are in a rainstorm. What words does the author use to create this feeling?

◎ Which words does the author use to make the rainstorm seem angry? Shy? Sad?

◎ What are some rhyming words the author uses in the book? How do these add to the feeling?

Poetry Pause

▲▲▲▲▲▲▲

Share a delightful poem about rain (below), then ask children what they think the author means by "it pattered all around the house" and "it found an open window and left tracks across the sill." Invite children to share ways they think the rain can be like a mouse. This is a good time to introduce the term simile (a comparison using *like* or *as*), explaining that the author of the poem is using similes in her descriptions. Some children will be able to understand exactly what a simile is; others will benefit from beginning to hear the term. Invite children to compare rain to other things as well, using the first line of the poem as a sentence starter ("The rain was like _____").

Rain Poem

The rain was like a little mouse,
quiet, small, and gray.
It pattered all around the house
and then it went away.

It did not come, I understand,
indoors at all, until
it found an open window and
left tracks across the sill.

—Elizabeth Coatsworth

Tip

▲▲▲▲▲▲

Rainstorm Patterns

Let children experiment with creating patterns using the rainstorm sounds (floor-slapping, knee-slapping, hand-clapping, finger-snapping, and hand-rubbing)—for example, using two sounds to create a simple AB or ABBA pattern.

Make a Rainstorm (Math)

With children sitting in a circle, try creating a rainstorm in the classroom.

◎ Begin by having one child rub his or her hands together to make the sound of rain gently beginning to fall. Have the first child "pass" this motion to the next child, who passes it to the next child, and so on, until all children are rubbing their hands together.

◎ Next, pass finger-snapping around the circle, followed by gentle hand-clapping, louder knee-slapping, and finally, the loudest: hands slapping the floor, to reproduce the sound of heavy rain.

◎ Finally, the rainstorm can gently begin to subside by doing all the motions in reverse: floor-slapping, knee-slapping, hand-clapping, finger-snapping, and hand-rubbing. (At this point children are making each sound as a group. When they get to the first sound again—rubbing hands together—they can drop off one by one around the circle, until one child is left rubbing his or her hands together, and then, finally, no sound.)

Raindrop Science (Science, Math)

Children discover properties of water by experimenting with drops of water on different surfaces.

◎ Set up a center with the following materials: Copies of the reproducible data collection mini-book (pages 24–25), water droppers, plastic cups (with water), waxed paper, paper towels, sandpaper, plastic plates, sponges, and food coloring (optional).

◎ Have children slowly drop water on the surface of each material (waxed paper, paper towel, sandpaper, plastic plate, sponge). Encourage them to observe how the water behaves on the different surfaces. For example, ask, "Do the drops stick together?" (Note: For the sake of visibility, you may want to tint the water with a few drops of food coloring, making it easier for children to count the drops of water.) Have children record their observations in the mini-book.

◎ Invite children to choose a new material to test, and record results on page 7 of the mini-book. Then have them complete page 8 to tell something they learned about water drops and something they still wonder about.

Rain Graph (Science, Math)

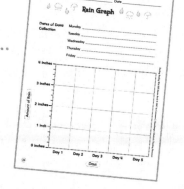

This activity reinforces graphing and measurement skills as children measure rainfall.

◎ Place a clear graduated cylinder or beaker outside, in an open area away from buildings and trees.

◎ Each day at the same time, have children measure the rainfall and empty the beaker, leaving it again for the next day.

◎ Give each child a copy of the graph (page 26) to record rainfall over a period of time (one week). Use additional copies of the graph to extend the data collection. Guide children in using their data to draw conclusions: Which was the rainiest day this week? Which was the rainiest week this month? Least rainy? Was this surprising? If children measured rainfall for the following month, what do they think they would find out? Have them test their ideas.

Word Play

The rhythmic language in this story makes readers feel as if they should grab an umbrella and get out of the rain! It begins with a "drip-drop tinkle," then a "tiptoe pitter-patter," and finally a "sounding pounding roaring rain" of a storm. To extend your After Reading discussion (page 21) take a closer look at ways the author uses words to create the feeling of a rain storm.

● Reread the story, using expression and varying your inflections and intonation to capture the intensity of the storm—from the "first whisper of the rain" to the "thunder-crashing" and, as the storm fades away, the "quietude" of "after rain."

● On a sheet of chart paper, list the words the author uses to describe the rain. Encourage children to play with and add to the words to create their own rainstorm with words.

● To go further with the language in this lively story, introduce onomatopoeia. Let children practice saying this big word. Explain that it means a word with a sound that makes you think of its meaning. For example, *buzz* is the sound we make to indicate a buzzing noise, and also the word we use to describe the sound. Reread *Listen to the Rain*, asking students to listen for examples of onomatopoeia (*drip-drop, tinkle, pitter-patter, splish, splash, splatter, mishy, mushy*).

Book Links

Bringing the Rain to Kapiti Plain: A Nandi Tale
by Verna Aardema
(Dial Press, 1981)

The arid Kapiti Plain is in desperate need of rain, so Ki-pat, a cattle herdsman develops a plan for bringing the rain to Kapiti Plain. Vibrant illustrations and cumulative rhyming text tell this gentle, memorable story.

Come On, Rain
by Karen Hesse
(Scholastic, 1999)

Tessie bemoans the heat wave that has gripped her city, as she watches cats pant and heat waver off tar patches in the alleys. When a very welcome rainstorm finally hits her city, Tessie dances with her friends.

Rain
by Peter Spier
(Doubleday, 1981)

This wordless picture book beautifully captures the essence of rainstorms and the children who play in them.

Rain Makes Applesauce
by Julian Scheer
(Holiday House, 1964)

This 1965 Caldecott Medal winner celebrates the wonder of childhood and silly talk. Enchanting, detailed illustrations add to this well-loved favorite.

Raindrop Science

Name _____

Date _____

1

What happened to the water drops on waxed paper? Draw a picture.

The water drops _____

_____

_____ .

2

What happened to the water drops on paper towels? Draw a picture.

The water drops _____

_____

_____ .

3

What happened to the water drops on sandpaper? Draw a picture.

The water drops _____

_____

_____ .

4

What happened to the water drops on a plastic plate? Draw a picture.

The water drops _____

_____

_____ .

5

What happened to the water drops on a sponge? Draw a picture.

The water drops _____

_____

_____ .

6

What happened to the water drops on _____ ? Draw a picture.

The water drops _____

_____

_____ .

7

Something I learned about water drops:

_____

_____

_____

Something I still wonder about water drops:

_____

_____

_____

8

Rain Graph

Dates of Data Collection

Monday _____

Tuesday _____

Wednesday _____

Thursday _____

Friday _____

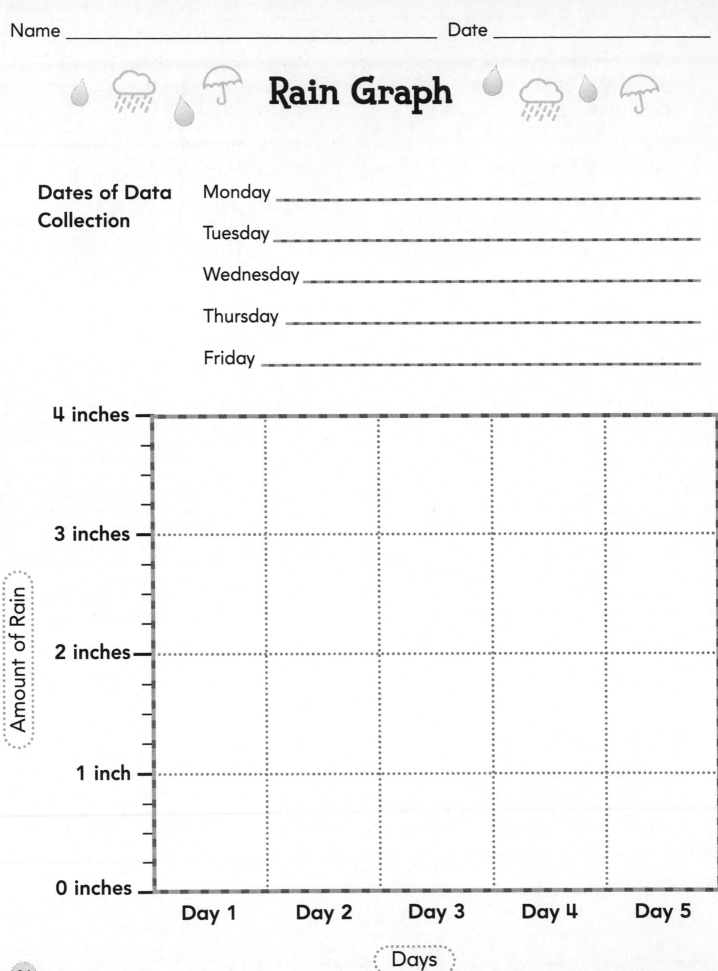

Amount of Rain

4 inches —

3 inches —

2 inches —

1 inch —

0 inches —

Day 1   Day 2   Day 3   Day 4   Day 5

Days

Teaching Reading With Bill Martin Books © 2007 by Constance J. Leuenberger, Scholastic Teaching Resources

Chicka Chicka Boom Boom

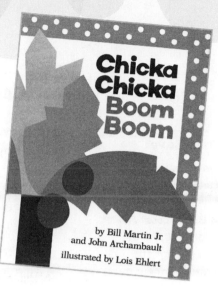

by Bill Martin Jr
and John Archambault
illustrated by Lois Ehlert

(SIMON AND SCHUSTER, 1989)

"**A** told B and B told C, 'I'll meet you at the top of the coconut tree.'"
And so begins the rollicking classic *Chicka Chicka Boom Boom*.
All the letters from A through Z climb atop the coconut tree until... "Oh,
no! Chicka chicka... BOOM! BOOM!"—the letters come tumbling down!
The uppercase letters then help the lowercase letters back up the tree.
Magical cadence and foot-tapping rhyme make this classic hard to put
down! For a younger version of this book, share *Chicka Chicka ABC*
(Simon Schuster, 1993).

Before Reading

Mischievous Letters

Show children examples of uppercase and lowercase letters. Ask
children what they know about these letters—for example, which
uppercase letters do they recognize? Lowercase? Explain to students
that this story is about a bunch of letters that get into some trouble.
Ask students to pay close attention to see how the uppercase letters
help the lowercase letters.

After Reading

Invite students to share their views of these playful
letters. Revisit pages in the book as students discuss
the role of each letter.

◎ How did those mischievous letters get into trouble?

◎ Do you think the author and illustrator intended for the
   reader to think these letters were children or adults? How do
   you know?

Tip

▲▲▲▲▲▲

ABC...123

Pair this book with its companion
Chicka Chicka 1, 2, 3 (Simon and
Schuster, 2004). Young readers will
recognize the cut-paper art and
lively story line, but in this case,
they'll count along as numerals
race to the top of an apple tree,
only to encounter a swarm of
bumblebees, which sends the
numerals tumbling backward. See
suggestions throughout these
pages for adapting the activities to
use with *Chicka Chicka 1, 2, 3*.

Tip

▲▲▲▲▲▲

Class Participation

Make it easy for children to join in
on the story. Give each child a letter
sign. Reread the story, encouraging
children to stand and hold up their
sign when they hear you say their
letter. Each time you read "Chicka
chicka boom boom! Will there be
enough room?" invite all children
to join in. Repeat with *Chicka
Chicka 1, 2, 3*, simply replacing the
letter signs with numeral signs.

ABC Center   (Language Arts)

This activity will entertain children while reinforcing letter recognition concepts.

◎ Cover a cookie sheet with brightly colored contact paper.

◎ Copy and color the coconut tree pattern on page 31.

◎ Place the coconut tree on the magnetic sheet and cover with clear contact paper. You now have a transportable literacy center!

◎ Add magnetic letters to the cookie sheet center and invite children to explore with the magnetic letters, matching uppercase and lowercase letters, spelling words, and more!

◎ Adapt the above directions to create a second center to support teaching with *Chicka Chicka 1, 2, 3*. Use an apple tree instead of a coconut tree, and provide magnetic numerals for exploration. Children can arrange the numerals in order, use them to create number sentences, and so on.

Chicka Chicka Boom Boom, Look Who's in Our Room!

(Language Arts)

Reinforce letter concepts and name recognition with this mini book.

◎ Give each child a copy of the mini-book cover (top half of page 32). Make enough copies of the bottom half of page 32 so that children can have one page for each letter in their name. Have children count out the pages to match the number of letters in their name, add the cover page, and staple to bind.

◎ Have children complete the rhyme on each page using the letters of their name (one letter per page). For example, Renee would write *R* on the first page, *E* on the second page, and so on, until she spelled her name.

◎ Invite children to paste or draw a picture of themselves on the cover of their book.

◎ Display the books in the reading center for children to enjoy.

Tip

▲▲▲▲▲▲

Time-Saver

Rather than create the cookie sheet literacy center, you can pick up the version of *Chicka Chicka Boom Boom* (Little Simon, 2002) that comes with a magnetic backing and magnetic letters.

Tip

▲▲▲▲▲▲

Play Alphabet Games

To go further, invite children to play alphabet games with the mini-books. For example, have children sort the books according to whether or not their names have letters in common with classmates' names. They can also sort the books by number of letters in the names, or number of syllables they hear when they say each name. To reinforce alphabetizing skills, have children place the books in alphabetical order (by first letter only).

Letter Patterns (Math, Language Arts)

This activity reinforces patterns while helping children practice letter recognition.

◎ Use letter-shaped sponges to make letter patterns on sentence strips. For example, one sentence strip may have the pattern A B A B A B A B; another sentence strip may have the pattern of G C C L G C C L.

◎ Give children a tub of letter tiles or magnetic letters and invite them to reproduce the patterns, laying the letters on top of the sponge-painted letters.

◎ To adapt this center for use with *Chicka Chicka 1, 2, 3*, replace the letter patterns with number patterns.

Chicka Chicka ABC (Language Arts)

Turn your classroom into an alphabet jungle with this attractive bulletin board.

◎ Help children tear and roll brown paper grocery bags to create a tree trunk and branches on a bulletin board.

◎ Cut out large green construction paper leaves. Sponge-paint one letter of the alphabet on each leaf with bright citrus colors, as depicted in *Chicka Chicka Boom Boom*.

◎ Send home one leaf with each child. Have children find something small at home that begins with the letter on the leaf. With permission, have them glue or staple it on the leaf.

◎ When children bring their leaves back to class, staple them to the branches on the tree. Encourage children to "read" the tree—saying the name for the letter on each leaf and the word for the object that represents it.

Tip

▲▲▲▲▲▲

Lakeshore Learning Materials carries an adorable fabric Chicka Chicka Boom Boom tree complete with letters that stick to the tree. The tree is weighted at the bottom and freestanding. (lakeshorelearning.com; 800-778-4456)

Book Links

**April Bubbles Chocolate:
An ABC of Poetry**
compiled by Lee Bennett
Hopkins
(Simon and Schuster, 1994)

This collection features a
poem for each letter of the
alphabet, making it ideal
for the young reader.
Langston Hughes, Carl
Sandburg, and Myra Cohn
Livingston are among the
contributors.

John Burningham's ABC
by John Burningham
(Random House, 1993)

Beautiful illustrations walk
the young reader through
the letters of the alphabet.

Quentin Blake's ABC
by Quentin Blake
(Knopf, 1989)

Using bouncy, rhyming
text, Blake charms us all
the way through the
alphabet with such
memorable verses as "M is
for Mud that we get on our
knees / N is for Nose—and
he's going to sneeze!"

Sleepy ABC
by Margaret Wise Brown
(Lothrop, 1953)

As night falls, all creatures
prepare for sleep. Lambs in
the field close their eyes, a
kitten yawns, and a young
child gets a goodnight kiss,
all as the letters of the
alphabet are lovingly
introduced.

Chicka Chicka Boom Boom Game (Language Arts)

As children play this fun game, they build letter recognition, listening, and
oral language skills.

◉ Write each letter of the alphabet on an index card.

◉ Write the words *Chicka Chicka Boom Boom* and draw a coconut tree on
four or five additional cards.

◉ Shuffle and stack the cards.

◉ Gather children in a circle. Take the first card from the stack. Hold it up
and say the letter (the sound, too, if children are ready, and later, a word
that starts with that letter).

◉ If you select a Chicka
Chicka Boom Boom card,
everyone gets up, wiggles
their hips, and says, "Oh no!
Chicka Chicka Boom
Boom!" and then sits back
down.

◉ Pass the stack of cards to the
child next to you, and have
that child repeat the process.

Word Play

Is there anyone who can read *Chicka Chicka Boom Boom* without tapping their
feet and being swept into the rhythm of the book? Capitalize on this feature as
you encourage children to experiment with the language of the book.

● This story begins "A told B and B told C, 'I'll meet you at the top of the coconut
tree.'" As the story continues, a question is repeated: "Chicka chicka boom
boom! Will there be enough room?" Invite children to chime in on the words
they know, chanting the words with the cadence of a jump-rope rhyme or using
different voices and tones for more fun with the language.

● Invite students to try their hand at making up some "cool cat" rhymes like the
one that follows. Can they think of any that would be perfect for this book?

> **Skit skat skoodle doot,
> Flip flop flee.
> Everybody running to
> the coconut tree.**

ABC
Center

Chicka Chicka Boom Boom, Look Who's in Our Room!

Place picture here.

Name

A B C

Chicka chicka boom boom!

Will there be enough room?

Here comes

Up the coconut tree!

The Happy Hippopotami

(HARCOURT, 1991)

Climb aboard the picnic buses for a happy hippoholiday! Come along as hippo mammas and poppas and their children enjoy a relaxing beach day: sunning themselves, eating goodies, dancing around the maypole, and even rocking to their steel guitars. A ton of fun is had by all!

Before Reading

Beach Day!

Lead a discussion about beaches to access students' prior knowledge. Encourage students to share what they know, based on pictures, books, visits to a beach, and other sources. Ask: *What kinds of things might you see at a beach? What types of things do people do at a beach?* The more information students can recall about the beach, the more they will enjoy the book!

After Reading

Point out the liberties the author takes to make words rhyme in the book, by making up such nonsense words as "Happy hippopotamights" and "hippopotaprizes." Explore word choice by revisiting and discussing passages with nonsense words:

◎ Why do you think authors make up words sometimes?

◎ What other words would have made a rhyme in these places?

◎ Do you think the nonsense words make the story more interesting or fun to read? Why?

◎ Do you know other authors who use nonsense words in their writing? How are their books like this book? Different from this book?

Beach Day
by Karen Roosa
(Clarion Books, 2001)

Explore all the components necessary for a perfect beach day: good food, good friends, and great surf!

Curious George Goes to the Beach
by H. A. Rey
(Houghton Mifflin, 1999)

Curious George and the man with the yellow hat have a great time at the beach, until the seagulls fly away with something valuable.

George and Martha Tons of Fun
by James Marshall
(Houghton Mifflin, 1980)

Hippo friends George and Martha celebrate their friendship in five short stories.

Those Summers
by Aliki
(HarperCollins, 1996)

Aliki shares vivid memories of summers past spent on the beach with her family.

Acting Like Hippos (Drama)

Children love to act out their favorite books, and this one offers just the right format for a class skit! Dramatizing offers many opportunities to build reading skills. As children dramatize story events, they interpret the characters' actions and thoughts, explore mood, and make connections. This book is easily acted out with no props, but if you want to extend the activity, enlist the help of students to make simple props (such as painted hippo masks from paper plates, brooms depicted as guitars, and beach supplies).

◎ Divide the class into groups of hippos based on the book (so you will have some hippopotamamas, hippopotapoppas, and so on).

◎ As you reread the story, ask each group to act out its part.

◎ To go further, invite groups of children to act out a plot extension (what might have happened before or after this story took place).

Postcards From the Beach

(Language Arts, Art)

Postcards are a playful way to provide practice with friendly letter-writing skills. Postcards are fun—through words and pictures they often share happy moments in new places. And the format of postcards provides a built-in opportunity for children to illustrate their words. Children will love writing postcards to describe the hippos at the beach. Follow these steps for helping children write their postcards:

◎ On chart paper, write a sample postcard. Review parts of a friendly letter: a heading (with sender's name and return address as well as date), a greeting (Dear Grammy), the body (what the message is), the closing (Sincerely, Love, Your Friend), and the signature. Keep in mind that most postcards will need only the date in the heading, not the return address.

◎ Give each child a copy of the postcard pattern (page 36). Have children fold the postcard at the center and tape or glue it closed.

◎ Invite students to pretend they were on the beach the day the hippos arrived. Have them write a postcard to someone special telling about what they saw. Then have them draw a picture that shows the beach.

Sinkers or Floaters? (Science)

With all those hippos diving in the water, children are bound to wonder, *Would they sink or would they float?* Let children experiment with the idea of sinking or floating with this fun activity. After, they can use what they learned to make their own predictions about whether a hippo would sink or float.

◎ Gather together several items that will sink or float, such as a rock, sponge, ruler, cork, wooden block, and any other items you have readily available in the classroom. Ask students to predict which items will sink and which will float. Encourage them to explain their thinking.

◎ Next, have children test each item in a container of water and then sort the items by whether they sink or float.

◎ Guide children to understand that objects sink or float depending on their density: Things less dense than water float, while things more dense than water sink. (Though density is a difficult concept for young children, they will, through their hands-on explorations, begin to build a foundation for later understanding.)

Do Real Hippos Act This Way?

(Science, Language Arts)

Lead students in a discussion that encourages them to compare real hippos with the hippos in the book.

◎ Check for background knowledge by asking questions regarding what real hippos eat, how they spend their time, and where they live.

◎ Give each child a copy of page 37. Invite pairs of children to research hippos and record facts they learn.

◎ Then have children record the same information for the hippos in the book.

◎ Let children share what they learned, and then compare it to the hippos in the book.

Word Play

You can just envision the hippos at the beach with playful lines like this from *The Happy Hippopotami*:

Happy hippopotami
On the sunny beach do lie
Like a stretch of granite boulders
Except, of course, for sunburned shoulders.

Encourage children to create their own playful descriptions with hippo words—for example:

Happy hippopotacylists
Ride around on cool bicyclets
Popping wheelies hippo style
Riding on for miles and miles.

Postcards From the Beach

Front of postcard: Draw a picture.

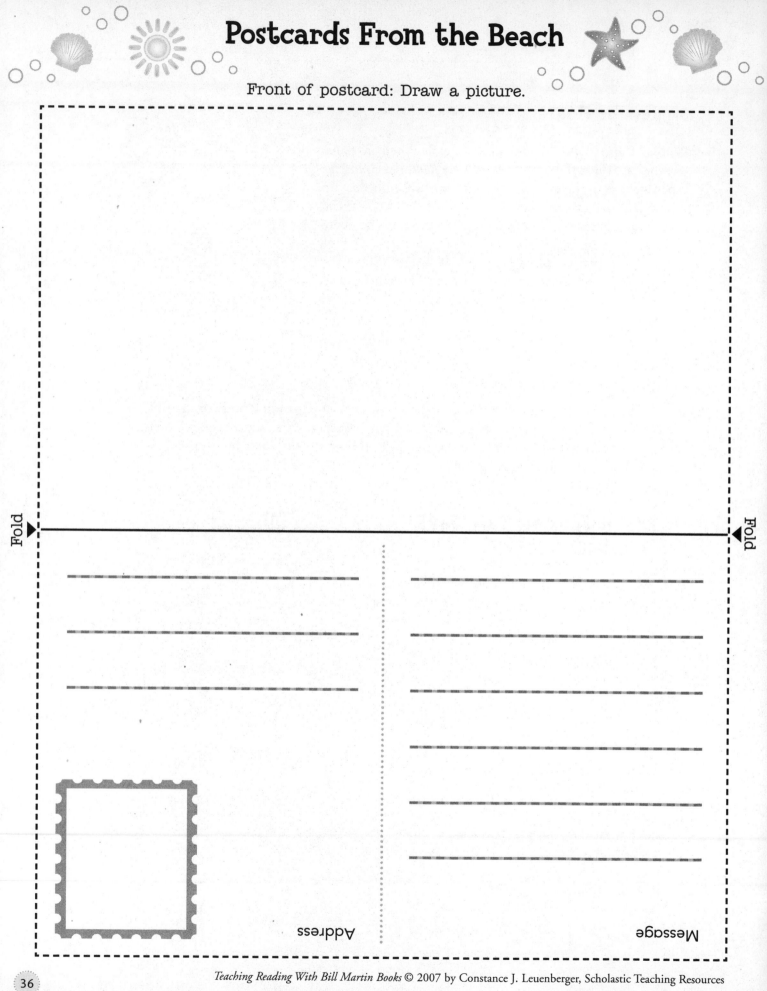

Fold

Fold

Address

Message

Do Real Hippos Act This Way?

	The Happy Hippopotami	Real Hippopotami
Where the Hippos Live		
What the Hippos Eat		
How the Hippos Spend Their Day		
Two Interesting Things About Hippos		

Teaching Reading With Bill Martin Books © 2007 by Constance J. Leuenberger, Scholastic Teaching Resources

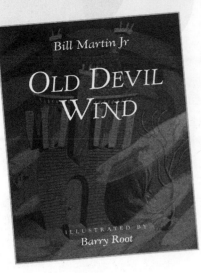

Old Devil Wind

❖❖

(HARCOURT BRACE, 1993)

This is a good old-fashioned spooky story that begins "One dark and stormy night Ghost floated out of the wall and he began to WAIL." As the cumulative tale continues, the entire scary house is rollicking with frightful antics, until the wind begins to blow, blowing away the ghost and all his menacing cohorts.

Before Reading

Chain Reactions

Invite children to tell what they know about chain reactions. Explain that a chain reaction is something that happens that causes something else to occur. Share that this story is about a ghost that starts a chain reaction, creating other spooky events. Invite students to find all the scary things that the ghost started in the story with just one wail.

After Reading

This is a great book to read on a dark and stormy day! Guide children in making connections to the story by asking these questions:

◉ Do you like scary stories?

◉ Why do you think the author wrote this spooky story?

◉ Have you ever heard another story that has the same beginning? Why do you think this story begins with "One dark and stormy night…"?

◉ How do you feel on a dark and stormy night?

◉ What do you think would be another good way to begin a spooky story?

Poetry Pause

▲▲▲▲▲▲

Share a shivery poem. Write the poem "Something Is There," by Lilian Moore, on chart paper (maintain the stair-step format shown). Invite children to tell what they notice about the poem. Discuss why they think the author chose the stair-step format for the poem. Let children try their hand at writing their own stair-step poems, or a poem in another shape.

Something Is There

Something is there
   there on the stair
      coming down
         coming down
            stepping with care.
         Coming down
           coming down
              slinkety-sly.

Something is coming and wants to get by.

—Lilian Moore

A Scary Puppet Show (Language Arts)

For some spine-tingling fun, try acting out the story with puppets! Using puppets to dramatize stories lets children learn more about characters and events and deepen their understanding.

◎ Copy and cut out the puppet patterns (page 41).

◎ Have students color the puppet patterns and glue them to craft sticks.

◎ As you reread the story, have students use the puppets to act it out.

◎ To reinforce literacy skills, including retelling, place the puppets and a copy of *Old Devil Wind* in the reading center. Invite children to use the puppets during center time to act out the story.

Story Strips (Language Arts)

An accordion book unfolds like the story in a book—one page at a time— making it a great format for a retelling. As children make accordion book retellings of *Old Devil Wind*, they will practice sequencing skills as they think about the major events in the story. An accordion book format also makes it easy to display children's work, encouraging them to revisit and retell the story again and again, strengthening comprehension and oral-language skills.

◎ Precut 9- by 12-inch sheets of white construction paper in half lengthwise. Give each child three halves.

◎ Have children tape the paper together end-to-end to make one long strip.

◎ Help students accordion-fold their strips into 12 equal sections.

◎ On the top section, have students write the title of the book (*Old Devil Wind*).

◎ Have children fill in the remaining sections with pictures of each item in the book, starting with the ghost and ending with the wind.

◎ Let children use their books to practice retelling the story.

Word Play

"One dark and stormy night..." Many scary stories begin with this opening line. Invite children to close their eyes as you read this line, and then ask: "What do these words make you think of or feel?" Encourage children to try their own hand at writing scary stories beginning with those five infamous words.

Tip

▲▲▲▲▲▲▲

Add props such as a witch's hat and magic wands. The wands work great as pointers for young readers.

Book Links

In a Dark, Dark Wood:
An Old Tale With a New Twist
by David A. Carter
(Simon and Schuster, 1991)

This book's dramatic build-up to the end where a large pop-up ghost jumps out is a thrill for children who like to be just a teeny tiny bit scared.

In the Haunted House
by Eve Bunting
(Clarion, 1990)

Follow the footsteps of two visitors through this haunted rhyming book. Each page is filled with yet another spooky surprise.

The Little Old Lady Who Was Not Afraid of Anything
by Linda Williams
(Thomas Y. Crowell Co., 1986)

Children will revel in the delicious scariness of this cumulative and humorous tale!

Pumpkin Eye
by Denise Fleming
(Henry Holt, 2001)

Vivid, eye-catching illustrations enliven this rhyming Halloween book. Large, simple text is perfect for early readers.

Haunted Reading House (Language Arts)

A haunted house stocked with plenty of scary stories and poems will have children reading nonstop.

- Obtain a large appliance box (appliance stores will usually give you theirs). Cut out windows and a door.

- Let children decorate the box to create a haunted house.

- Stock the house with scary stories and poems. (See Book Links, left.)

- Invite children to read spooky stories in the haunted reading house!

Ghost Hands (Art, Language Arts)

Children love an opportunity to create some ghosts of their own! These ghosts star in children's own spooky stories.

- Give each child a sheet of black construction paper.

- Place white tempera paint in a shallow container (such as a pie plate). Guide children in placing the palm of each hand in the paint and then stamping it on the construction paper.

- Let the paint dry, then have children glue on wiggly eyes (at the palm end of their prints). Have children turn their handprints upside down to discover a couple of very cute ghosts (that also serve as a record of children's small hands).

- Invite children to write (or dictate) a story about their ghosts. To get them started, revisit the beginning of *Old Devil Wind.* (See Word Play, page 39.)

Teaching Reading With Bill Martin Books © 2007 by Constance J. Leuenberger, Scholastic Teaching Resources

Bill Martin Jr   Vladimir Radunsky
THE MAESTRO PLAYS

The Maestro Plays

❖

(HENRY HOLT, 1994)

Stunning, bold illustrations picture the maestro playing "proudly" and "loudly" as he marches through this vibrant picture book. As the maestro rides an elephant, he plays "reachingly" and "flowingly, glowingly, knowingly, showingly, goingly" while charming a group of snakes. The clownlike maestro continues through the book until the concert ends in "BRAVO!"

Before Reading

Maestro's Music

Invite children to share their experiences with music. Have they ever been to a concert? Do they play a musical instrument themselves? What is their favorite music to listen to? Tell students that this book is about musical instruments and the different sounds each instrument makes. Explain that a maestro is a master of an art form. The maestro in this story is the leader of a group of musical performers.

After Reading

Discussion Starters

After sharing the story, revisit the illustrations with children to explore the idea that, along with the text, illustrations can help readers better understand the story.

◎ Guide children to notice that some illustrations are horizontal and some are vertical. Ask: "What do you notice about these illustrations? Why do you think the illustrator chose to make the illustrations this way?"

◎ How do the colors and shapes in the illustrations help tell the story?

◎ What are some ways the illustrations help tell what's happening in the story? For example, children might notice how the art helps show how the maestro is playing ("proudly," "loudly," "dizzily," "wildly," and so on).

Poetry Pause

▲▲▲▲▲▲

Share this poem about a band. Then invite students to act out the poem as you reread it.

❀

Here Comes the Band

The band comes booming down the street,
The tuba oomphs, the flutes tweet tweet;
The trombones slide, the trumpets blare,
The baton twirls up in the air.
There's "oohs!" and "ahs!" and cheers and clapping—
And I can't stop my feet from tapping.

—*William Cole*

Musical Paintings (Art, Language Arts, Music Appreciation)

This interactive art activity will get children's creative juices flowing—and provide a playful opportunity to build vocabulary for descriptive language.

◎ Using brightly colored paints (use the book for inspiration), invite children to paint as they listen to selections of music. (The music from *Peter and the Wolf* is a good choice for young children.)

◎ Ask children to paint in time to the music, using smaller or larger strokes depending on the tempo and sound of the music.

◎ When the paintings are finished, give children sentence strips. Have them write (or dictate) words to describe their paintings. They can use words from *The Maestro Plays* for inspiration.

◎ Have children glue their sentence strips to their paintings. Invite children to share the words they chose to describe their paintings and tell why they go together.

Here Comes the Band (Art, Music Appreciation)

Children love to play musical instruments! Gather some common household materials to make some fun instruments.

◎ Partially fill an empty plastic soda bottle with dried beans and uncooked rice (hot-glue the top on) to make a great shaker.

◎ To make maracas, fold a paper plate in half and place dried beans and uncooked rice (or unpopped corn) inside. Staple around the edge to seal. (For a more festive instrument, staple crepe paper streamers or ribbon around the edges.)

◎ Stretch rubber bands across an empty tissue box to create a string instrument.

◎ Use empty coffee cans for drums and lids from cooking pots for cymbals.

◎ Read aloud the story as children play along on their instruments.

◎ Place the instruments and the book in a center, and encourage children to make music as they retell the story.

Tip

▲▲▲▲▲▲

Children always enjoy finding out what the older kids in a school are up to. If there are older children in your school who play instruments, invite them to visit your class and share their instruments. Encourage them to play a short piece for the class and to answer questions about their instruments.

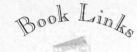

Book Links

Charlie Parker Played Be Bop
by Chris Raschka
(Orchard Books, 1992)

This infectiously rhythmic story makes readers feel as if they are actually listening to music.

Meet the Orchestra
by Ann Hayes
(Gulliver Books, 1991)

This fact-filled book is set at an evening at the symphony, beginning with the audience and the musicians preparing for the big night.

Thump, Thump, Rat-a-Tat-Tat
by Gene Baer
(Harper and Row, 1989)

"Thump, thump, rat-a-tat-tat..." A marching band parades through this book, with bright, bold colors and the title's repeating sound pattern.

Zin! Zin! Zin! A Violin
by Lloyd Moss
(Simon and Schuster, 1995)

This Caldecott Honor book playfully introduces each instrument in a classical orchestra, while at the same time teaching music appreciation.

Big Sounds, Little Sounds
(Language Arts, Music Appreciation)

Invite children to try this fun activity that encourages musical appreciation and enhances word choice.

◎ Give each child a copy of page 45. Ask children to look at the picture of each instrument. Ask: "Do you think the [name each instrument in turn] has a big or little sound?"

◎ In the center column, have children write sound words (as in *The Maestro Plays*) to match what they think each instrument sounds like.

◎ Next, play a few selections of music that feature each instrument—for example, "Peter and the Wolf," by Sergei Prokofiev. (This piece was written especially for children to introduce the sounds of an orchestra.) After listening, ask children to complete the page with new words that go with each instrument. Encourage a discussion about what children discovered. For example, ask: "Did you guess which instruments had a big/little sound? Was it easier to think of words before or after listening to the music?"

Word Play

Silly, nonsense words and special text features add to the playful feel of *The Maestro Plays*. The first page "booms" with loud, capital letter words:

> "THE MAESTRO PLAYS.
> HE PLAYS PROUDLY.
> HE PLAYS LOUDLY."

Each successive page features an illustration that depicts the feel of the music. Some pages need to be turned sideways to capture the full illustration. Try these activities to extend the playfulness of this book's language:

● Revisit the book, looking at each illustration and the type of words chosen for each page. Explore placement of words on the page, type size, use of uppercase and lowercase letters, and so on, to make connections to the musical feeling the author is trying to convey.

● Have children create new pages for the book, using features they explored as a guide to decide on word size, placement, and so on.

Name _____   Date _____

Big Sounds, Little Sounds

Instruments	Big Sound or Little Sound?	Sound Words
Tuba		
Violin		
Flute		
Trombone		
Drums		
Piano		
Clarinet		

Teaching Reading With Bill Martin Books © 2007 by Constance J. Leuenberger, Scholastic Teaching Resources

The Turning of the Year

✦✦

(HARCOURT, 1998)

Word Play

"**I**n January, out I go to welcome winter's icy blow. In February, bound with snow, I sled the hillside, top to toe." *The Turning of the Year* is filled with rhyme sequences for each month. Invite students to explore the melodious language with their own month-by-month poems:

● Have students use the rhymes in the book as inspiration for writing poems about their birthday month. Students with birthdays in the same month can work together. If a month is not represented, come up with the rhyme as a class.

● On chart paper, record children's poems in sequence.

● Read the poems aloud, exploring children's word choice and rhyme.

Each month and season is joyfully celebrated in this book as children sled, splash, chase fireflies, pick pumpkins, and more. Heartwarming illustrations add to the feeling of the book, making this a great read-aloud any time of the year!

Before Reading

Seasons of the Story

Before reading the story, invite children to name the seasons. Let them share some of their favorite activities in each season of the year. Encourage discussion about the changing seasons, and invite children to explain how they know when one season turns to another.

After Reading

Does this book make children long for a certain season? Poetic text and evocative illustrations capture the months beautifully. Encourage children's attention to the details with these questions.

◎ What is your favorite month in the book?

◎ What words did the author use to show some ways this month is special?

◎ What details can you find in the illustration that show what is special about this month?

◎ Did any of the words or illustrations about a certain month surprise you? Why?

Rhyme-and-Read Fluency Builder (Language Arts)

Noticing rhyming text helps young readers develop appropriate phrasing, an important component of fluency. Students will enjoy reading aloud the poetic text in *The Turning of the Year* again and again, with repeated practice fostering fluent reading.

◎ Choose a favorite month in the book and read aloud the rhyming text. Write the text on chart paper (or a whiteboard) and underline the rhyming words at the end of each line. Read aloud the verse again, tracking the text on the chart paper, and emphasizing the rhyming words. Explain to students that noticing rhyming words as you read helps you develop a rhythm to your reading. Circle punctuation marks (commas, periods). Explain that this punctuation also helps you be a better reader: It shows you where in the text to pause.

◎ Invite children to join in on a repeated reading of the rhyming text you selected. Then set up a center for students to practice reading aloud their own favorite rhyming lines from the book. Provide a copy of the book, a tape recorder if possible, and sticky notes. Let students visit the center in pairs. Have them select a favorite month and practice reading the text aloud together and to each other. Students can give each other feedback on their readings, for example, noticing whether their partners emphasized rhyming words or paused at a comma. Children can tape record and critique their readings, noticing what they do well and what they want to pay more attention to in a repeated reading.

◎ Have children write their names on a sticky note and place it on the page they practiced reading. Later, invite students to share their reading with you. Notice ways in which students use pacing, intonation, and expression.

Poem of the Month (Language Arts)

Children love learning and memorizing new poems. Introduce them to a new one each month with this fun activity!

◎ Each month, share a poem that children can memorize if they wish. To encourage children in their efforts, select poems with a manageable length. Poems that rhyme may also assist children in memorization.

◎ Copy the poem on chart paper and read it aloud. Repeat the poem, inviting children to chime in. Reread the poem with children throughout the month, and encourage them to practice reciting it with partners.

◎ Invite children to copy the poems into special books. (Staple paper together to make the books.) If children are unable to copy, provide them with photocopies they can add to a binder. When children memorize a poem, give them the honor of reciting it to the principal. Children love this privilege, and it's a great way to share what is going on in your classroom.

Tip
▲▲▲▲▲▲▲

Keep kids chuckling month after month with poems by Douglas Florian, winner of the 1995 Lee Bennett Hopkins Poetry Award. His short, playful poems are just the right length for young children to learn. A few favorite collections follow:

Beast Feast (Harcourt, 1994)

Bing Bang Boing (Harcourt, 1994)

Insectlopedia (Harcourt, 1999)

Summersaults (Greenwillow, 2002)

For more poems by Douglas Florian, plus activities that build reading and writing skills, see *Teaching With the Rib-Tickling Poetry of Douglas Florian* by Douglas Florian and Joan Novelli (Scholastic, 2003).

Book Links

A Child's Calendar
by John Updike
(Knopf, 1965)

Updike's beautiful yet simple imagery paired with Hyman's irresistible illustrations make this a book you'll want to celebrate all year long.

Everett Anderson's Year
by Lucille Clifton
(Holt, 1974)

Everett Anderson is a seven-year old African-American boy whose life in the city is recorded in verse through each month of the year.

My First Book of Time
by Claire Llewellyn
(DK Publishing, 1992)

This comprehensive study of time—from digital clocks to months of the year—has a very user-friendly format with bright primary colors.

When the Frost Is on the Punkin
by James Whitcomb Riley
(Godine, 1991)

Written from a young farm girl's point of view, this endearing poem uses dialect to tell its story.

Tip

▲▲▲▲▲▲▲

Get moving to the Macarena! Join Dr. Jean and boogie with the "Macarena Months"—a fun and active way to learn the months of the year! Find Dr. Jean and the "Macarena Months" song on the CD *Dr. Jean and Friends.* (drjean.org)

Step Into Seasons
(Math, Language Arts)

Children will become more familiar with the seasons when they make this fun "step" book.

◎ Stack two sheets of standard copy paper as shown, lining up the bottom edge of the top sheet about one inch above the sheet below.

◎ Fold the top of the papers back to create four staggered pages. Staple along the fold.

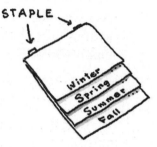

◎ For each book, write "Winter" along the bottom of the top page. Along the bottom of the next page (the strip of the page that shows) write "Spring." Repeat with the final two pages for "Summer" and "Fall."

◎ Invite children to use words and pictures to tell about each season.

Keepsake Books (Language Arts, Math, Science, Social Studies)

These unusual books reinforce calendar concepts while serving as a reminder of the activities that happen each month.

◎ To make the books, give each child 12 envelopes. Instruct children to write (helping those who need it) the names for the months on the front of their envelopes (one month per envelope). Bind each child's book with an O-ring.

◎ At the beginning of each month, invite children to decorate the corresponding envelope. Throughout the month, encourage children to place items in the envelope that represent special events, activities, learning, and other things they want to remember.

◎ For months children are not at school, consider sending home a note to families, along with the books, suggesting that they complete the books with their children at home as a way of keeping memories of their time together.

A Beasty Story

(HARCOURT, 2002)

"In a dark, dark wood there is a dark, dark house..." This spooky tale will have children squealing with delicious fright as mice follow a beast into a dark brown house, down the dark red stair, into the dark blue cellar, into the dark purple cupboard, and through other creepy, colorful places, and eventually out into the dark, dark night! This is a wonderful story for reinforcing word recognition for colors.

Before Reading

Shivery Stories

Help students understand that cadence helps to build suspense while reading a scary story. Ask:

◉ What kind of voice would you use to tell a scary story?

◉ What do you think is the best way to read a scary story—fast or slow? Why?

◉ How can slowing down when I read aloud a scary story make it seem scarier to you?

◉ Can speeding up in some places ever make a scary story seem scarier? How?

◉ What keeps you on the edge of your seat when you are listening to a scary story?

After Reading

Encourage discussion of character and setting with these prompts:

◉ Is there something scary about a character in this book?

◉ Where does the story take place? Is there something scary about this place?

◉ Which part of the story is the scariest? What happens to make this part scarier than other parts of the book?

◉ Did you feel "deliciously" afraid (a little afraid, but kind of fun!)?

Creating Your Own Beasty Story (Language Arts)

Using *A Beasty Story* as a model, create a class-made scary story. Use chart paper and a shared or interactive writing approach to encourage student participation at all levels.

◎ Invite children to suggest a beginning for the story. They may want to start off the same way as the book, or they may have their own ideas about how to begin a scary story. Write the beginning on the chart paper, using the opportunity to teach features of language or standard writing conventions. For example, if children choose to begin the story, "On a dark, dark night...," you might point out the beginning of the sentence (capital letter) and use the word *dark* to reinforce the variant vowel /är/ phonogram.

◎ Let children take turns adding on to the story. Look for opportunities to involve children in writing the story on chart paper. Based on children's developmental writing level, this can be as simple as having them write the first letter of words that begin with the same letter as their first name or writing the end of a word to practice a familiar spelling pattern.

◎ When the story is complete, divide it into sections for children to copy onto drawing paper. Let children illustrate their sentences and then put their pages together to make a book.

In a Dark, Dark Bag (Science, Language Arts, Creative Thinking)

This fun activity will get students using their senses, and building vocabulary for descriptive words!

◎ Line several brown paper lunch bags with plastic bags. Trim the plastic bags to size and staple the inner and outer bags together at the top.

◎ Gather several items that have distinctive shapes and textures—for example, grapes that have been peeled (the feeling resembles eyeballs!), strands of cold cooked spaghetti, and gelatin. Place each item in a bag.

◎ Bring children together in a seated circle. Pass the bags around and invite children to place their hands in the bags without looking. Ask children to describe what they feel.

◎ After everyone has had a chance to explore each bag, discuss what might be inside.

◎ Reveal the contents of each bag and discuss children's guesses. Ask: "Was your guess close? What clues did you use?"

"Dark, Dark Color" Mini-Book

(Language Arts)

Children can create their own spooky mini-books using the text pattern in *A Beasty Story* for writing support.

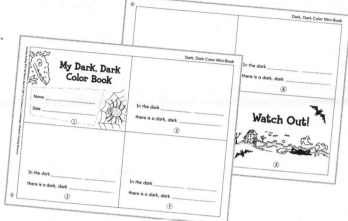

◉ Give each child a copy of the mini-book template (pages 53–54).

◉ Have children write a color word and a noun (something that names a person, place or thing), in the first two blanks and a noun in the last blank of each page (2 through 7).

◉ Invite children to illustrate their pages and then pair up to share their stories.

A Spooky Treasure Hunt (Critical Thinking, Following Directions)

Send children on a spooky hunt that reinforces listening and thinking skills while providing practice in following directions. Turn down the lights to add to the effect!

◉ Using the text pattern in the book, create a set of directions for locating a spooky surprise in the classroom. Sample directions follow:

1. In the dark, dark classroom there is a dark red shelf.

2. On the dark red shelf there is a dark brown box.

3. In the dark brown box there is a dark green box.

4. In the dark green box there is a dark purple case.

5. In the dark purple case there is a ghost!

◉ Plan ahead so that children find the surprise after following the final direction.

◉ Children can team up to prepare new sets of directions (with a surprise at the end) for their classmates to follow.

Tip

▲▲▲▲▲▲

To make a simple, small ghost for children to find at the end of their spooky hunt, cover a few cotton balls with a white tissue. Tie a string around the tissue to create the ghost's "head." Glue on wiggly eyes. Other fun surprises include plastic spiders (also black cats and vampire teeth), jack-o'-lantern erasers, tiny (plastic) black cats or vampire teeth, a new scary story to read aloud, and a spooky message painted in red paint.

Book Links

A Dark, Dark Tale
by Ruth Brown
(Dial, 1981)

"Once upon a time there was a dark, dark moor. On the moor, there was a dark, dark wood. In the wood there was a dark, dark house." This spooky tale will hold little listeners' attention until the last spooky page!

In a Dark, Dark Wood: An Old Tale With a New Twist
by David A. Carter
(Simon and Schuster, 1991)

A pop-up ghost at the end of the story makes this favorite story even spookier. This is a great read-aloud for those who enjoy a fright!

Scared Silly! A Halloween Book for the Brave
compiled by Marc Brown
(Little, Brown, 1994)

This collection of scary stories actually helps young listeners laugh at their fears right along with friendly ghosts and playful monsters!

Happy Hauntings! (Math)

This spooky but fun activity reinforces math concepts as children shiver with fright and delight at tales of ghosts and jack-o'-lanterns.

◉ In advance of using this activity, prepare dried lima beans (or other counters) as follows (each child will need 10 to 20). On half of the lima beans, use a fine, permanent marker to draw ghost faces. (See sample, right.) Spray paint the remaining lima beans orange and, when dry, use the marker to draw jack-o'-lantern faces on them.

◉ Give each child a copy of the haunted house pattern (page 55). Invite children to color and decorate their haunted houses before the math lesson.

◉ Give each child a handful of lima beans (both ghost and jack-o'-lantern faces). Share scary number stories, and have children manipulate the ghosts and jack-o'-lanterns on the haunted house to solve the problems. For example, you might say, "Three ghosts lived in a spooky house. The ghosts decided to decorate their house for Halloween and brought home four jack-o'-lanterns. How many ghosts and pumpkins are there all together?"

Word Play

Repeated words (such as "dark, dark") in *A Beasty Story* create a playful rhythm in the text. Invite students to think of other adjectives that, when repeated, help to describe something, and create a catchy phrase. Use the book *The Teeny-Tiny Woman*, by Paul Galdone (Clarion, 1993), to explore a different way catchy strings of adjectives paint pictures in readers' minds. For example, the author writes "Once upon a time there was a teeny-tiny woman who lived in a teeny-tiny house in a teeny-tiny village." As the story continues, he builds on the teeny-tiny theme, creating suspense and predictable text. Students can try some of their own—for example: "In the huge, huge barn, there was a huge, huge tractor…," and so on.

My Dark, Dark Color Book

Name _____

Date _____

1

_____ In the dark

there is a dark, dark _____ .

2

_____ In the dark

there is a dark, dark _____ .

3

_____ In the dark

there is a dark, dark _____ .

4

In the dark _____

there is a dark, dark _____ .

⑥

Watch Out!

⑧

In the dark _____

there is a dark, dark _____ .

⑤

In the dark _____

there is a dark, dark _____ .

⑦

Name _____ Date _____

Happy Hauntings!

KEEP OUT!

I Pledge Allegiance

(CANDLEWICK 2002)

"Allegiance is loyalty." "A pledge is a promise." Using simple explanations, this informative book emphasizes the importance of the Pledge of Allegiance, while explaining the history and significance behind each line. This book is a great teaching tool for young children learning the Pledge of Allegiance, bringing meaning to those hard-to-understand words.

Before Reading

Patriotic Primer

Ask students what they think the Pledge of Allegiance means. What does it mean to pledge something? What does the flag represent? Elicit from children questions they may have concerning the Pledge of Allegiance and the American flag, and encourage discussion. Return to these questions as you read the book aloud and children discover answers to some of their questions.

After Reading

This book is chock-full of information. Discuss with children some of the things they learned from the book. Use the following prompts to encourage discussion:

◎ What information surprised you?

◎ How did the illustrations make you feel?

◎ How does this book make you feel about our flag?

◎ What is something you know now that you didn't know before we read this book?

◎ What do you still wonder about the Pledge of Allegiance?

Create a Flag (Language Arts, Social Studies)

Use this cooperative learning activity to give children a chance to design their own flags for their classroom or school.

◎ Divide the class into small groups (three or four children per group).

◎ Have each group design a school or class flag. Provide pictures of flags around the world for inspiration.

◎ Encourage children to pay special attention to the colors and patterns they choose for their flag, giving thought to why each color and pattern is significant to their classroom or school.

◎ When each group has finished planning and sketching their flag, have children create a finished flag on a large sheet of drawing paper.

◎ Display the flags as a reminder of what is important to your class or school.

Flag Cake (Math, Science)

Reinforce math and science skills while making this yummy flag cake.

◎ Following the directions on a boxed cake mix, allow children to measure and pour the ingredients to make a cake.

◎ After the cake has baked and cooled, spread white frosting on it.

◎ Invite children to decorate the cake to look like a flag, using red licorice sticks as the stripes (the white frosting will be the white stripes).

◎ For the union, use blueberries spaced evenly so that the white frosting shows through for the stars.

◎ Celebrate Betsy Ross's contribution to our country with a cake party!

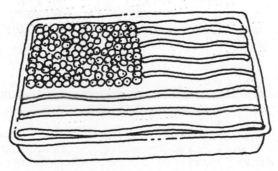

Tip

▲▲▲▲▲▲

Did You Know?

Did you know that the Pledge of Allegiance was originally written just for children? It was written by Francis Bellamy and first published in a Boston-based magazine entitled *The Youth's Companion* on September 8, 1892. Bellamy was a chairman of a committee of the state superintendents of education. As a chairman he was preparing a program for the public school celebration for Columbus Day, and so he wrote the Pledge of Allegiance in its original form: "I pledge allegiance to my flag and the Republic for which it stands, one nation, indivisible, with liberty and justice for all." In 1954 an act of Congress added the words "under God" to the pledge.

Book Links

America the Beautiful
by Kathleen Lee Bates
(Putnam, 2003)

This is a pictorial tribute to the endearing song, with illustrations that invoke the American spirit.

The Pledge of Allegiance
by Francis Bellamy
(Cartwheel Books, 2001)

The words of the Pledge of Allegiance are illustrated with powerful photographs.

Stars and Stripes: The Story of the American Flag
by Sarah L. Thompson
(HarperCollins, 2003)

Double-page spreads feature simple and clear text about the history of the flag and bright, full-page illustrations.

This Land Is Your Land
by Woody Guthrie
(Megan Tingley, 1998)

Woody Guthrie carries his guitar from California to the New York island in this beautiful picture book that depicts the landscape of America in oil paintings and multipaneled spreads.

Old Glory (Art, Language Arts, Social Studies)

The art in *I Pledge Allegiance* is very unique in its torn-paper collage style. Invite students to create their own flags, imitating this style of illustrator Chris Raschka.

◎ Provide red, white, and blue construction paper and glue.

◎ Ask children to create a replica of an American flag by tearing pieces of red, white, and blue construction paper and gluing them to a larger sheet of paper.

◎ Invite children to explain (they can write or dictate) what the United States flag means to them.

◎ Display the flags and statements, sharing and discussing them as a class.

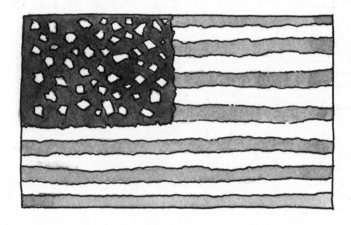

Word Play

"No matter how much we might disagree about some things, we all agree on one thing: We are strongest when we stick together and help each other out." Passages like this interspersed throughout *I Pledge Allegiance* help children understand the meaning of this important part of American history. Try these activities to bring attention to the words on each page:

● Revisit the book, looking at the placement of the words on each page. Explore how the placement of words helps readers better understand the text.

● Different font sizes highlight the words of the Pledge of Allegiance and the explanations of those words. How can you tell which words are part of the Pledge of Allegiance and which are the explanation? Do the authors make it clear? How?

Trick or Treat?

(SIMON AND SCHUSTER, 2002)

A young Dracula and his mother go trick-or-treating on Halloween. As they visit each floor of his apartment building, Dracula is given a bundle of treats, until he reaches the tenth floor. There, Magic Merlin plays a trick making everything "WACKBARDS!" As Dracula revisits all of his previous stops, he is given the same treats, just backward! Jelly Beans become "Belly Jeans" and Chocolate Sticks turn into "Stocolate Chicks." When he arrives back home again, he is greeted with a hug from his father, breaking the WACKBARDS! spell.

Before Reading

Trick or Treat?

Show children the cover of the book and ask them why they think there is a question mark at the end of the title. Remind children that question marks are used at the end of questions. For fluency practice, let children practice reading the title, using the question mark as a clue for expression. Then discuss why the title is a question. Did the author intend to make readers wonder if the boy in the book will get tricks or treats at Halloween? Ask children what they think they will get when they go out trick-or-treating on Halloween: Tricks or treats?

After Reading

The distinct descending text pattern in this book makes it a natural for children to recognize patterns in reading. As you reread the beginning pages, invite children to point out the patterns they notice in the book.

◎ How did the author make readers feel that he was really moving from floor to floor?

◎ What helps make this book suspenseful? (Guide children to notice how the pattern "travels" from one floor to the next.)

◎ How does the pattern help readers make sense of the story?

Poetry Pause

▲▲▲▲▲▲

Give each child a copy of the poem "The Folk Who Live in Backward Town," by Mary Ann Hoberman (page 62). Invite children to explore the poem with these questions: Which lines [words] of the poem describe what the people of Backward town are like? Which tell how they live? What are some other things you think the people in Backward town might do? How do you know? How are their lives the same as yours? Different? What are some things you might like to do in Backward town? Why?

Wackbards! (Language Arts)

A Halloween cauldron filled with treats is the basis for this activity.

◎ Fill a large pot (such as a plastic cauldron you might find at a party store) with small treats.

◎ Gather children in a circle and place the cauldron in the center. Reveal some of the contents to children.

◎ Next, choose a child to use a magic wand (any wand or stick will do) and wave it over the cauldron. Now tell children everything is WACKBARDS!

◎ Let children take turns choosing a treat from the cauldron and giving it a "wackbards" name. For example, using the book as inspiration, gummy bears might become "bummy gears." Spell the name for the treat—in both its forward and wackbards form—on chart paper. Children will enjoy reading their word list, forward and wackbards!

Little Ghosties and Ghoulies (Math)

Children get so excited around Halloween and love to talk about the costumes they will be wearing on the big night. Turn that enthusiasm into a math lesson.

◎ Make a large graph of many general descriptions of costumes, such as scary, pretty, TV or movie character, funny, job, and other.

◎ Invite children to place a graph marker (a Halloween-themed marker is always fun, such as a pumpkin cutout) in the costume category they would choose for Halloween.

◎ Follow up the graph activity with math-based questions, such as: "How many children want to be [category]? In our class, would we have more [category] or [category]?"

Wackbards Day! (Language Arts, Creative Thinking)

Choose a day to celebrate as Wackbards Day. Explain to children that Magic Merlin has put a spell on the class and now everything must be done wackbards.

- On this special day, invite children to come to school wearing a piece of clothing backward.

- Reverse the day's routine, beginning with activities that normally fall at the end of the day.

- During the day, do many of the normal activities backward, such as reading books from back to front and writing backward stories.

- Wrap up the day by writing a class account of how it felt to do everything backward.

Word Play

Children will have fun getting tongue-tied as they say the names of the trick-or-treater's neighbors in this story.

- List the neighbors' names on a sheet of chart paper (Knicker Knocker, Slipper Slopper, Wiggle Waggle, and so on). Then list their "backward" names (Totter Teeter, Thamble Thimble, Pickle Pumper, and so on).

- Invite children to read the names—first forward, then backward.

- Challenge children to say the names quickly in sequence. What happens?

- Point out that creating silly rhymes that leave readers tongue-tied is one way that the author is playing with language to keep readers interested.

Book Links

Halloween Poems
compiled by Myra Cohn Livingston
(Holiday House, 1989)

Short, shivery, and very scary poems make up this collection of Halloween horrors.

Six Creepy Sheep
by Judith Ross Enderle and Stephanie Gordon Tessler
(Caroline House, 1992)

As six creepy sheep venture out on Halloween night, they quickly begin to "turn tail with a shriek" until one by one the party dwindles. In the end sheep, pirates, and other Halloween pranksters meet for a rollicking Halloween party.

Trick or Treat, Smell My Feet
by Diane de Groat
(William Morrow, 1999)

When Gilbert the opossum and his sister accidentally exchange Halloween costumes, the fun begins! Gilbert finds himself squeezing into a pink tutu instead of his Martian space pilot costume. In the end, it's all about being a good sport and being flexible.

The Folk Who Live in Backward Town

The folk who live in Backward town
Are inside out and upside down.
They wear their hats inside their heads
And go to sleep beneath their beds.
They only eat the apple peeling
And take their walks across the ceiling.

— by Mary Ann Hoberman

Pretend you live in Backward town. What do you do?
Draw a picture. Write a sentence.

Teaching Reading With Bill Martin Books © 2007 by Constance J. Leuenberger, Scholastic Teaching Resources

Celebration of Learning

Celebrate children's learning by wrapping up your Bill Martin Jr. author study with a Bill Martin Jr. celebration. Invite students to make invitations to the celebration. In the spirit of the work of Bill Martin Jr., encourage them to use poetic language in their invitations. After the invitations are sent home, let the celebration begin with these enriching and playful activities.

Look What We've Done!

Display children's completed work from the author study. Students can decorate different areas of the room to depict Martin's books, and place related work at each. One corner might be scary, to reflect the theme in *A Beasty Story* and *Old Devil Wind*; another might be a beach scene from *The Happy Hippopotami*. Create a poetry center to display children's poetry notebooks (page 8). Students can entertain their guests here, reading aloud from their poetry and Martin's books, such as *Listen to the Rain*.

Tip

Display at the reading corner Martin's books along with accompanying tapes or CDs for students and their guests to enjoy together.

Sugar Cookies

2 1/4 cups flour

1/4 teaspoon salt

2 teaspoons baking powder

1/2 cup butter

1 cup sugar

2 eggs

1/2 teaspoon vanilla

1 tablespoon milk

Cream sugar and butter, then mix in eggs and vanilla. Combine dry ingredients and add to butter mixture, along with the milk. Roll out the dough and cut into animal shapes. Bake for approximately nine minutes, or until lightly browned, at 375° Fahrenheit.

Story Snacks

Prepare snacks to share that represent various books. For example, make the Flag Cake from the lesson on *I Pledge Allegiance* (page 57). Or try these Animal Cookie Characters, based on *Brown Bear, Brown Bear, What Do You See?* (page 9). Before eating these treats, children can use the cookies to share a dramatic retelling with their guests.

◎ Mix up a batch of sugar cookies (see recipe, left).

◎ Roll out the dough and use cookie cutters shaped like the animals from *Brown Bear, Brown Bear, What Do You See?* to make the cookies. Bake as directed, and let cool.

◎ Mix food coloring into prepared frosting to decorate the animal cookies.

◎ Let children act out the story with their cookie characters, then eat them up!

Martin and Math

Display all graphs completed over the course of the study in one area of the classroom, then invite guests to work with students to create new graphs.

◉ Display each Martin book and provide a "ballot" box or bag.

◉ Invite guests to drop a scrap of paper in the box or bag identifying their favorite books.

◉ Use the data to create a graph of favorite Bill Martin books.

More Books by Bill Martin Jr.

In addition to the 12 stories featured in this book, Bill Martin Jr. has written and coauthored dozens of others. What better way to celebrate than by sharing additional titles to enjoy. Gather books and place them in baskets at the literacy center. Invite children to choose a favorite to share with a guest. Or gather everyone around for a read-aloud.

THE GHOST-EYE TREE
(Holt, Rinehart and Winston, 1985)

Children will relish this spooky tale of two siblings who embark on an errand on a dark and windy night.

POLAR BEAR, POLAR BEAR, WHAT DO YOU HEAR?
(Henry Holt, 1991)

This twist on *Brown Bear, Brown Bear, What Do You See?* challenges children to listen to what they hear.

A BEAUTIFUL FEAST FOR A BIG KING CAT
(HarperCollins, 1994)

A clever mouse taunts a conceited cat with visions of a feast fit for a big king cat, until the end when the mouse is outsmarted.

THE WIZARD
(Harcourt, 1994)

A wizard and his assistant friends playfully cast rhyming spells that unexpectedly result in calamity.

FIRE! FIRE! SAID MRS. MCGUIRE
(Harcourt Brace, 1996)

In this hilarious adaptation of an old nursery rhyme, Mrs. McGuire (a news anchor) is alerted to a fire downtown, which is followed by an amusing chain of events.

SWISH!
(Henry Holt, 1997)

The Cardinals and the Blue Jays are in the final minute of their girls' basketball game. Martin uses his trademark rhythmic language to narrate the highlights.

LITTLE GRANNY QUARTERBACK
(Boyds Mills Press, 2001)

Granny Whiteoak, a star quarterback in her younger days, hears that her team needs her. Despite obvious ailments, she springs from her bed and takes off to save her team!

CADDIE THE GOLF DOG
(Walker, 2002)

When Jennifer's dog runs away, he finds a home with boys who name him Caddie because of his ability to catch golf balls. Later, when Jennifer makes a phone call to inquire about a puppy, she gets a happy surprise.

PANDA BEAR, PANDA BEAR, WHAT DO YOU SEE?
(Henry Holt, 2003)

Following Martin's *Brown Bear, Brown Bear, What Do You See?* style, readers meet a zoo full of new characters.